12 UNDENIABLE LAWS FOR MARRIAGE

WHAT THE BIBLE SAYS THAT CAN MAKE YOU A WORLD-CLASS MARRIAGE

BY: TIFFANY DOMENA

TABLE OF CONTENTS

PREFACE

This book is not an exhaustive guide to every potential marriage problem that you may have seen or experienced in life. This book is not going to make your marriage a cakewalk. Your marriage will require effort, and will reap the effort that you sow into it. This book is not a bashing party to degrade your husband or your wife, so DO NOT use it that way. Do not nitpick at the words of this text and say to your spouse, "Honey, I read in this book that you are doing this wrong and should change it". If you are here and you are reading this text, this book will provide you with the laws to improve your perspective on marriage, and instruct you of how to pay attention to the actions that can stimulate a better (even world-class) marriage. This book can have more effective results if both parties are willing to place effort into implementing the principles, however, it will still be useful if a married individual reads the text and implements its context alone.

A world-class marriage is one worthy of admiration from all over the world. It is a marriage that has an overwhelming aroma of love, and attracts the curiosity of viewers who ask, "How do they love each other so much?", "How do they maintain that level of enthusiasm to be together?", or "How don't they manage to get tired of being around one another?" A world-class marriage is not simply an exterior illusion, but it is a fulfilling relationship between two people who have not only fallen in love, but also committed to stay in love. It transcends physical, emotional, intellectual, social, and spiritual stimulation. Marriage can simultaneously fulfill every sense and every realm of humankind; enabling every fiber of being to be invigorated. No other institution or relationship can provide the same refreshment as does marriage when fidelity has protected its potential. A world-class marriage is not an impossibility, but the effort must be in agreement with the desire.

Happiness is a possibility of marriage. Joy can be increased in marriage. Peace can be multiplied in marriage. However, there are laws that you must abide by to achieve the happy marriage of your dreams. This book is a compilation of wisdom that I have accumulated from intense reading, personal experience, and observation as I have been able to witness three generations of happy marriages in my family. In this book, you will find laws that (when persisted upon) will enable you to nurture and develop a world-class marriage.

Within this text are:

- 12 Laws That Can Reverse The Momentum of ANY marriage and get you on your way to a world-class marriage

- Questions that will inspire growth of your Character

- Action Steps To Push You Closer To Your Potential As An Individual And As A Couple

- Stories To Subconsciously Reprogram Your Mind

- And, Prayers That Will Manifest Heaven On Earth

INTRODUCTION

As a young girl, I loved Barbie and Ken. I had a fond ability to make great love stories for them, and they all had happy endings. Playing with Barbie, playing house, or any of the other imaginative acts whereby little girls and boys imitate the possibilities of adulthood always depicted happy stories, but the wisdom of how to achieve them is a rare commodity. The reality of the world today is that most marriages fail, and majority of the marriages that stay together do so with extreme dissatisfaction; the happy stories of our childhood imagination are rarely found in the adulthood reality.

One delusion of life is that in every historic period, intense training has been maintained to defend physical territories, but spiritual territories as sacred and longstanding as marriage do not have nearly as intense the basic training or accountability. In 2006, I went thru Basic Military Training where I learned all of the values that I must set aside to defend my country (a physical territory). To defend my country, The United States Of America, I must be willing to guard the rights of the Constitution even to the extent of sacrificing my life. Billions of soldiers across the world have dedicated their loyalty, passion, time, and lives to defend physical territories and virtues.

The staple of mankind is marriage. Marriage is the institution that provides stability to the world. Thru healthy marriages, children are born in stable homes with the vibrational uplifting of both male and female; providing them with a balanced outlook on life. Thru marriage, love, joy, peace, patience, gentleness, kindness, and self-control are multiplied in others at a rate that is otherwise impossible. Beyond the defense of a country, marriage transcends physical territories, and provides the greatest offering and benefit of any institution in the world.

The same passion and fight that won the American Revolution and the World Wars must be the same spiritual and emotional diehard passion in your marriage. Committing to your marriage does bring personal fulfillment, but the bigger picture is that you are protecting the hopes, faith, and possibility of generations to engage in the staple institution of mankind. You must have a completely self-yielding, self surrendering zeal infused to prevail the ego and exterior circumstances, and sustain a happy marriage. For this reason, the Bible says, "Husbands, love your wives, just as Christ also loved the church and gave Himself for her". In war, people were willing to sacrifice their lives for a freedom that they may never be able to enjoy, but they fought despite the facts. Do you want a world-class marriage? If so, you must be willing to confront the necessary sacrifices to reap the greatest harvest that society bears witness to; an unending, lifetime companionship that cannot be found in any place other than marriage.

I look forward to spiritually walking alongside you as you flip thru the pages of this text, and transform your marriage for the better of you, your family, and our world.

May your marriage be blessed!

Tiffany Domena

Tiffany Domena

CHAPTER ONE

ALWAYS IMPROVE YOUR CHARACTER

"Confront the dark parts of yourself, and work to banish them with illumination and forgiveness. Your willingness to wrestle with your demons will cause your angels to sing."

— August Wilson

A wise man said, "Character is like smoke, you cannot hide it." You might pretend to be what you are not, or hide the nature of your true character for a while, but after a short time, it will be known. You cannot hide from yourself. Your character is a demonstration of who you are. You were created to reflect divinity, but at times, we choose otherwise. Yet in spite of the fact that you are demonstrated by your character, you can actually do something to improve and make it better.

The greatest room in the world is the room for improvement. So it is not an excuse whatsoever to say "take it or leave it; that's who I am." You can be better. There is room for improvement. And if you are not prepared or ready for improvement, then you are not ready to have a happy marriage.

The Story Of Pius And Tina

It was a beautiful Saturday morning; the sun had just risen out of its chamber with its ray of light and life filling the mountainous landscape of Egret, a little town, down south of Liberia. The long awaited dream of Tina was going to come true.

Tina had met Pius some 6 years before in a Christian fellowship on a college campus. For Tina, it was love at first sight. She had arrived a little bit late for the meeting, but the moment she entered the meeting hall, she met this young charming "brother" ministering the Word to the believers (about 20 of them) on that Wednesday evening. It was her first year in college; and how much she had prayed for God's guidance to meet and to marry a good Christian (preferably a preacher).

She had her hopes about his looks and disposition in her mind. And here she was, sitting in the second to the last row of the set of chairs arranged in the fellowship hall. She gazed at this young ebullient, handsome, and intelligent undergraduate. "He looks it. He talks it. He might be the one," she thought to herself. She quietly muttered a prayer under her breath; "Oh Lord if he is the one, let him be the very first to give me a handshake with a charming smile after the service tonight." And it was her first night in this fellowship.

She had trusted God to lead her to a good campus fellowship where she would be free to serve God, and where she would feel at home. "Maybe this young man would measure up with my fleece after the meeting is over," she thought. Typically, first-time visitors are treated with dignity, welcoming them into the fellowship.

True to her thought, Pius walked right down to her, and gave her a warm and friendly handshake. He gave her the smile of her life as he approached her to welcome her to the fellowship. "Yes, it is! My sign has come true," she muttered quietly.

12 UNDENIABLE LAWS FOR MARRIAGE

In the days and months that followed, Pius and Tina dated and courted. It was like heaven on earth for both of them as their friendship developed and grew into what looked like a "for better, or for worse."

When they graduated from college, they highly anticipated their marriage. They planned their wedding ceremony, and it turned out splendid. What a ceremony it was! The air was filled with love and the church filled with roses and music as the intending couple walked down the aisle to the altar to be joined as husband and wife.

"Today, I pronounce you husband and wife. And what God has joined together let no man put asunder," declared the pastor, presiding over the wedding. "And you may now kiss your bride." The applause resounded in the church hall and in the air when Pius walked slowly and closely to Tina to unveil and to kiss her; the first kiss of their marriage.

Now, the wedding has ended; life has begun. Three years down the line, and Pius is wondering, "Is this the woman I married. Lord, did I miss it?" Tina is wondering also in her heart, "I supposed I married a good Christian and a preacher at that, but why does he shout at me at the slightest provocation! He almost beat me up a few days ago even in the presence of our two kids."

Pius is the first born child of his family. He was raised to lead and to always be in control. His word was the law in his home growing up, and he expects the same in his home now.

Tina was the youngest child, and was showered with her every desire. She thought that every man was like her father, who always would compassionately allow her to do any and everything at home.

The marriage is under strain; its flavor and romance is gone. Things are falling apart between Pius and Tina. Both parties are contemplating a divorce or at least a break up in the meantime.

Maybe you can relate to Tina and Pius. When marriage begins, many people say that we are "blinded by love". The truth is that we typically assign love to conditions and with everyone on Earth being imperfect, our perceptions are imperfect, and our spouses are not able to live to the specifications that we perceive are "perfect". Even worse, no one is able to live to the perfection of God without continually striving to crucify their desires and submit to a relationship with Him. We are giving our spouses an impossible milestone!

In order to maintain a happy marriage, you must be willing to improve your character. Interaction with your spouse will reveal to you differences between the two of you. Neither difference can be considered right or wrong without the consultation of scripture. When you read scripture, you must FIRST take responsibility for your role in every situation. Taking personal responsibility in a conflict is the HARDEST thing to do.

I remember a time when someone had broken into my car. They had thrown my possessions around, they stole my checkbook, and they took change that I had in the car. I was upset because the car is mine, and the thief had no right to go into my car. However, I did not take responsibility for my role in the whole ordeal first. When I told my husband, he said, "Honey, did you lock the doors?". I said, "Honey, that doesn't matter. That does not give anyone a right to touch my property, but even worse, they went in, and took my possessions. Now, I have to waste time to 'Stop payment' on checks and replace other miscellaneous items".

Based on my story, my husband pointed out to me the part of the ordeal that I could control. I had not locked the doors on the car. The person did not have a right to touch my property, but I could have controlled what was within my power, and I had not. Additionally, I could have maintained my checks in another location, so that this possibility was not so easy. Even beyond the physical things that I could have done to ensure no tampering with my car, I could have put spiritual hedges around my property to ensure that the attack of Satan could not come close.

Situations like Pius and Tina reveal the power of character in marriage, and as I shared thru my story, character begins with self-responsibility. The humility to know and understand that your marriage will reveal imperfections in your character is the beginning of paramount construction in your life and in your marriage.

Commit To Your Marriage

A happy marriage is a creation that you commit to contributing to every second of the day. It is not a passive, autopilot activity. Similar to a potter spinning on the wheel, God has created us "good", and allowed us to share His goodness with companions, but we MUST decide every second of the day to demonstrate good character and create a great marriage. If you want more love in your marriage, sow seeds of love. If you want more kindness, sow kindness. I know that this is not easy, but your marriage depends on your effort to chisel away the imperfections of your character, so that you can be a greater demonstration of love. Unconditional love is your highest potential!

Be more patient

The Random House Webster dictionary defines patience as bearing provocation, annoyance, pain, etc., without complaint or anger. It says it is persevering and diligent; steady, able and willing to endure; that is what patience is. And to be candid with you, I must say that it is not easy to be that way. But if you are ready to have a happy marriage, worthy of emulation and inspiring to other people around you, you must be patient. Not only should you be patient, but you must continually improve on being patient. You can get better.

I remember the counsel that a church member gave me when I was about to get married to my husband. He said, "the only way for you to make this marriage work is to give one hundred percent. Forget when everybody tells you 50/50. Give one hundred percent without looking at what the other person is giving. Also, marriage requires that you practice patience." I have since found out that he was right. I cannot love or demonstrate good character on the basis of what or how the other person acts. I must crucify my own desires, and demonstrate the unconditional Spirit of God.

Be more kind

Take it or leave it, kindness is a virtue that is worthy of coveting if you want to create a happy marriage. The Scripture demonstrates kindness when it says, "God is kind, slow to anger and plenteous in mercy: The LORD is gracious and full of compassion, Slow to anger and great in mercy. The LORD is good to all, And His tender mercies are over all His works."[1] You see, it God's nature to be kind.

In other parts, the Bible expounds further on anger saying that it is foolish, and even more, you should stay away from hot-tempered people. Anger is a sign that wisdom is not present. Who wants to be known as a fool? It is up to you to choose within yourself how you will respond in circumstances that you do not understand or that strike your emotions.

I used to struggle with anger. Today, I have less common and more controlled episodes of anger. I have consciously worked to improve my actions and my reactions to situations to alleviate the tumultuous consequences of anger. I made an agreement within myself that when my thoughts begin to say, "Tiffany, do they know who you are", and my blood pressure begins to gush thru my veins that I would take captive my thoughts, remind myself of the good in every situation, and separate myself if the situation was too overwhelming to clear by lingering around. My practice works majority of the time. Practice wins championships, and so am I.

Kindness is a mandatory asset that must overwhelm good character. Someone who is kind behaves in a gentle, caring, and helpful way towards other people. He is of a good or benevolent nature. His disposition is compassionate. He is considerate or helpful.

Consideration is shown by understanding that your spouse has a different perception than you, and demonstrating an

---

1   Psalms 145:8-9 NKJV

understanding and interest in their perspective on matters. Consideration is also shown by giving equal priority and reverence to the other person's view as you do for your own. Consideration is KEY to kindness and must be demonstrated simultaneously in a happy marriage.

Be more forgiving

To err is human, but to forgive is divine. You bring yourself into the very class of God when you learn the act of forgiveness; it is the greatest thing in the world. Forgiveness is the greatest need in the world. It was for you and I to be forgiven that God sent Jesus. The very essence why God sent Jesus to die for humanity was such that He could offer us forgiveness of sins. If there is anything you have to learn to do to make a peaceful marriage, it is forgiveness. And don't forget that when God forgives, He forgets. You are the children of your Father God. Forgiveness should be your ongoing practice. Release expectations that limit you or your spouse to respond to the voice of God, and expect miraculous transformation every day and all the time.

Be more selfless

Did you know that the greatest problem in marriage and in the world at large today is the problem of self? In our society, we have self made millionaires, self help products, and the loud resounding media always says, "Take care of yourself....", planting a thought process of independence; rather than the interdependence necessary for success. Everybody wants to be independent. We have crowned "self" as Lord and King of our Society. The very forces that drive our civilization thrive on self. In response to united efforts, they say, "what do I stand to gain!" That evil has crept into families and marriages and is eating and destroying it as fast and as hard as cancer. Hey, child of God, if your marriage must work, you must let go of self. It doesn't mean losing your identity, but taking the attention off yourself to the other person, your spouse. Work at being more selfless.

Summary

- Always Improve Your Character
- Be more patient
- Be more kind
- Be more forgiving
- Be more selfless

Exercise One

Take a pen and write a pocket note-a 90 day forgiveness promissory note: "I forgive you every wrong you will ever do to me in this 90 day period, whether you ever apologize or not." Duplicate this into 3, and place one in your office, the other in your bedroom and the third in your suit pocket to carry about.

CHAPTER TWO

LEARN YOUR PURPOSE AS A COUPLE

"God has brought us together as families to bring to pass His eternal purposes. We are part of this plan in this marriage relationship. let us love and respect and honor one another. We can do it, and we will be the better for it."

— **Gordon B. Hinckley,** *Stand a Little Taller*

God is a God of order and purpose. Dr. Myles Munroe said that When the purpose of something is not known, abuse is inevitable. Don't you ever make the mistake of thinking that you met your spouse by chance or just for the fun of romance and sexual intercourse. Never! You met on purpose. God had a specific plan that can only manifest amongst the two of you.

The Story Of Adah, Vera, and Robert

Vera and Adah had a hard time growing up in the mountainous city of Jos; a plateau state. Their parents had separated when Vera was only three years old, and the mother had to raise them by herself. Growing up with both parents was tough, but growing up with a single parent even tougher.

The memories of her father beating his wife, and even abusing his children filled the mind of Vera. She unconsciously had taken every man to be that way. "Life is a game of chance, what it will be, will be." Vera had accepted this philosophy from her mother; a phrase she usually used to console herself.

Vera had grown up and gone to college. In college, Vera met Jesus and accepted him into her life as Lord and Savior. In her formative years, she had set her mind in a mole that could not be reformed in just a few years of walking with Christ. Two years later, Vera met and married, Robert, a preacher's son.

For Vera, life was a game of chance and what it will be, will be. For her, the place of the will and the purpose of God was laughable. "I do not believe in purpose but chances, she would say to Robert." "God is a God of order and purpose," Robert would throw back at her. "Everything is left to chance and God does not so much as care about what we do, not even our marriage. Whatever we are able to make out of it, fine, and whatever we are not, we would leave to chance. What is God's purpose if my father deserted us for another woman when I was only three-years-old? I do believe in God, but that He is particular about me and my marriage, I find it difficult to accept. I suppose we are free moral agents; and God gave us a will and allowed us to make choices for what we want whether good or bad."

The greatest need in Christendom today is the need for the renewal of the mind. Many people come into the body of Christ with their minds made up and fixed about certain issues and ideas that they have formed in their minds due to certain experiences and upbringing.

The truth is that no matter what anyone believes, if it does not align with the word of God, it is erroneous and a lie of the devil.

Jesus said that the Word Of God is truth.[2] "Let God be true and everyman, every circumstance a liar", said Paul. [3]

Regarding the marriage of Vera and Robert, many people can relate to their scenario, and you may see both sides as well. I want you to know some facts about God and his plan for your marriage.

God Has A Purpose For Your Marriage

God is particular about your individuality. It matters to him who you marry. He is interested in the minutest detail of your life even down to what you eat and wear, where you live and work. Jesus said, "Are not two sparrows sold for a penny? Yet not one of them will fall to the ground outside your Father's care. And even the very hairs of your head are all numbered. So don't be afraid; you are worth more than many sparrows."

He does not leave us to chance. He gave you options, and he knew the outcome of each of them. He has a purpose for marriage in general, but much more He has a particular purpose for your own marriage. Take time to open your mouth, and ask Him, "Father, what is the truth about my marriage? How can your Kingdom be manifested thru our union?" Find out what the purpose of your marriage is.

How a Marriage Can Affect the World

Let me tell you something; the greatest threat to the devil is your marriage. He knows that you being married to the man or woman of God will endanger his existence. For this reason, he

2 John 17:17
3 Romans 3:4

doesn't mind you missing it in marriage. He wants your marriage to fail, and unless you learn to fight, marriage will be much tougher than it has to be. Is it any wonder that the family, the Christian family in particular is his greatest hit in the world today? He is afraid that you would give to the world another Jesus, or another Ruth, or another Paul.

When I think of the awesomeness and wonders of marriage, the story of Joseph and Mary, the earthly parents of Jesus come to my mind. Imagine, if there was no Joseph and Mary, or that Joseph was not the kind of person that he was. What would have happened to the Son of God coming into the world? What would have happened to your redemption?

The marriage of Joseph to Mary has long changed the world for good. The devil is afraid that you might just be another Joseph and Mary; channels through which God will bring into the world again another seed that would bruise his head.

Marriage Is the Foundation of Creation and the World Society

The first institution ordained by God is marriage. God made one man from the dust of the ground, and made the woman out of the man. He saddled them with the privilege and reverential responsibility of bringing forth His dream children to fill the surface of the earth. The Bible says:

"So God created man in His own image; in the image of God He created him; male and female He created them. Then God blessed them, and God said to them, "Be fruitful and multiply; fill the earth and subdue it; have dominion over the fish of the sea, over the birds of the air, and over every living thing that moves on the earth."[4] Settle it in your spirit, without marriage between a man and a woman, there would be no society, and no civilization.

How You Can Discover Your Purpose as a Couple

If you want to know the purpose of a product, you ask the manufacturer. The person who discerned marriage must know the purpose of it. I would like you to understand that marriage was all God's idea; it originated from Him and not from man. So being a God of purpose, He must have something in mind that He ordained this institution. We know that He has not left us in the dark regarding the purpose for which He made it.

Now, let's go to the manufacturer's manual for the purpose for which the manufacturer instituted marriage. In Genesis Chapter Two, the Manufacturer gave the purpose for marriage: It says: And the LORD God said, "It is not good that man should be alone; I will make him a helper comparable to him."[5] Again it says: "So Adam gave names to all cattle, to the birds of the air, and to every beast of the field. But for Adam there was not found a helper comparable to him." [6]The word of God gives the purpose of your marriage.

Ephesians 5:23 says, "The husband is the head of his wife as Christ is the head of the church. It is his body, and he is its Savior." The husband was created to express divine dominion over the Earth (with the exception of mankind), and to direct his family as he follows God. He is called the head. In anatomy, the head

4   Genesis 1:27-28
5   Genesis 2:18
6   Genesis 2:20

is the leader and messenger of the human physical form. When we liken the man to the head of the physical body, we can shed light on God's intention for man in marriage, and God's intention for man in relation to Him. The head contains the brain which is the receptacle for human intellect. It is the first measurable operation that controls human thought and action. The Soul and Spirit cannot be measured aside from the effect on the physical body. Inspiration and revelation cannot be measured, but can be observed by studies of the brain. As the head, the man is the first responder to spiritual influence, and the one that passes messages thru the entire body.

The wife was made to be the helper to the husband. She was made to spice up his life, and is supposed to be submitted to the man as he is to God.

If you ask and fellowship with the Holy Spirit, He will lead you into the very purpose to which your particular marriage was fashioned. Invest in His friendship and you will find out, and because He does not change, it will be in line with Genesis Two verse eighteen and twenty.

Analyze Where Your Teamwork Works

Paul was very specific in the family stature of church leaders. The status of the home was directly correlated to effectiveness in church leadership. Regarding elders, he said, "An elder must be blameless, faithful to his wife, a man whose children believe and are not open to the charge of being wild and disobedient."

Marriage is about teamwork. The first member of that team is your spouse. And as every other concept, you must understand the principles guiding teamwork to run your most important team in the world. If you cannot manage your team at home, you will not be able to make the necessary decisions to manage teams outside of the home.

John C. Maxwell has this to say about teamwork: "Teamwork makes the dream work, but a vision becomes a nightmare when the leader has a big dream and a bad team." The greatest dream of a true spouse must be to raise his or her mate to where they can each carry out the dreams and passion of their hearts. However, in order for one to be able to do this, he must first study and know the spouse.

To understand the details of your spouse, you should be attentive to important details about them. Dr. John Gottman, author of The 7 Principles Of Making A Marriage Work called this "love-mapping". He said that you should be conscious of the circumstances that occur in your spouse's life: past and present.

Circumstances are tools that God uses to grow you and those around you. The story of Job tells us of circumstances that God permitted to take place in the life of Job simply to prove his reverence to Him. Job 1: 6-12 says:

Now there was a day when the sons of God came to present themselves before the Lord, and Satan also came among them. And the Lord said to Satan, "From where do you come?"

So Satan answered the Lord and said, "From going to and fro on the earth, and from walking back and forth on it."

Then the Lord said to Satan, "Have you considered My servant Job, that there is none like him on the earth, a blameless and upright man, one who fears God and shuns evil?"

So Satan answered the Lord and said, "Does Job fear God for nothing? Have You not made a hedge around him, around his household, and around all that he has on every side? You have blessed the work of his hands, and his possessions have increased in the land. But now, stretch out Your hand and touch all that he has, and he will surely curse You to Your face!"

And the Lord said to Satan, "Behold, all that he has is in your power; only do not lay a hand on his person."

So Satan went out from the presence of the Lord.

Your spouse is experiencing things everyday; some situations as a consequence to his/her free will and some as a result of association. Family lineage, leisure and work associations all cause circumstances as consequences to you and your spouse.

Additionally, your spouse is constantly changing. Our bodies evolve; from a baby-size corpse and actions to an elderly body and actions. As you evolve, your interests change, your tastes change, and your favorites change.

The Earth is constantly spinning. As a result, it is affected by the presence of the other stars and planets in space. The movement of the Earth affects the bodies of water that contain millions of trillions of gallons of water, the mountains are affected at tons of pounds, personalities, and civilizations are also affected as air mass coordinates, wind speeds vary, and light rays reflect differently.

Your spouse is alive, which means that they have expectations, desires, interests, things that they enjoy, colors that they find interesting, music that is calming, relationships that they are culminating, and dreams that have yet to be fulfilled. Find out who they are associated with, how that is benefitting their purpose, how you can help support their dreams and desires, and map the present circumstances that affect their lives. As you are getting more specific about the circumstances and interests of your spouse, you will find that their judgement is affected by their environment, their patience, their kindness, they may be influenced to act with more or less love as a result of their present circumstances. The influence of their environment does not make their circumstance right, however, it is good for you to know, so that you can discuss these matters, and gracefully make corrections as necessary. The Word of God is your most potent weapon when ungodly character or demonstrations manifest in your home or marriage. Find the scripture that gives details of how things should be, talk to the Manufacturer about the presence of a "virus" or "malware", and share the instruction that you hear from God. The Bible says:

"For the word of God is alive and active. Sharper than any double-edged sword, it penetrates even to dividing soul and spirit, joints and marrow; it judges the thoughts and attitudes of the heart."[7]

A person is one with emotions, intellect and will. Personality study is further enhanced by knowing the distinct temperaments that people are born with. With these kinds of studies and observation, you are able to know the strengths and vulnerabilities of your spouse; giving you greater ability to empower and support them. It is your duty to find out who your spouse is and then build a team from there.

---

7 Hebrews 4:12

Analyze Your Talents and How They Can Be Used To Accent One Another

No one is born handicap and deficient of talents and gifts. Even the physically challenged are bundles of talents and endowments.

You must find out what the gifts and talents of your spouse are, understand, harness, and compliment them. To understand their talents and unique abilities means to appreciate your spouse's' differences. You are different than everyone else on the Earth, and your spouse is too. Their interest may be rare, and difficult to understand how to monetize, but rather than speaking words of defeat, your responsibility is to support their desires by connecting them with others that can enhance what they already have. Couples are meant to complement each other.

It might surprise you to know that your wife's garrulity is an endowment from God that if well harnessed and channeled properly might make for her fortune. Strengths and talents are given to be manifested and used to support your daily bread. Do not worry how, but ask God, "How can we support our family with ....? Let your abundant Kingdom be manifested thru this now", and it will be done.

Analyze Your Areas of Increased Wisdom

The Scripture says that "Wisdom is the principal thing; Therefore get wisdom. And in all your getting, get understanding"[8]. There are things and areas that a person is endowed and good at. Find out what makes your spouse tick and fulfilled, and explore it together. There are some women who are good homemakers but

---

8 Proverbs 4:7

not good managers of funds. So it is wisdom to know what your spouse is most good at, and reinforce them in the areas that they are not. Wisdom knows what to do and does it.

Keep Your Marriage As An Example Of Infectious Love

Love has an aura; an aroma. When you enter into a home that is enwrapped in love, you know, you can pick it from the atmosphere. Love is divine and transcends language barriers and all other differences. You can also identify a home where hate and strife rule from the point that you enter. Love and hate are infectious. Even when you meet a couple who are pretending to be what they are not, you know. Love's aura is so strong that the physical and spiritual senses pick it up. Did you know that children know an environment where love exists and vice versa? They don't have to see you beating their mother to know. Even an infant in the womb (a fetus) senses love. But for you, your goal must be a home that is a haven of love and affection. Let people see you and your spouse and say," what an example of love".

Similar to when a bad smell comes or the temperature changes in a room, keep your senses alert for when the love is not flaming in the room. Ask yourself, "Are everyone's hearts and minds clear?", "Is there anything else that I can do to add more love into my home?", "How can I love or surprise my spouse more?", and stay open for the answers and the actions that arise.

Love Encourages

The thing about love that all of us must know is the fact that it looks for the strength of another and fans it to the flames. Yes, there is rebuke in love, but much more is that it encourages one to push on, try harder, and never to give. Do you suppose what it will mean to your spouse if after he returns from his office feeling beaten and disappointed, and you put your arms around him and say words like: "You are the greatest man in the world, you can make it. Why not try it this way, don't quit." It means the world to have such support from their spouse. While it is true that we all make mistakes, we all stay in situations until we outgrow them, and we all are affected by circumstances around us, seeing the good in every situation, and appreciating the positive in it can be of great appreciation to your spouse.

When I was in the military, I lost the zeal to do the exercises that were required. I have always been artistic and enjoyed dance or artistic motion, rather than running, pushups, and situps. At times, I would procrastinate, and workout right before my physical training test. My husband would always say, "Tiffany, why don't you go work out today. Jaelin can hang out with me." He even went as far as to volunteer to work out with me in the mornings before work, but I would give excuses. When it became really close to my physical training test, he would still express compassion and encourage me even though he understood that I procrastinated. Yes, he would tell me that I should plan to do different next time, but he would always close his rebuke saying, "You can do it, Honey. Put in more effort in focusing your mind or endurance, and you will be fine". His support meant so much to me. Despite my procrastination, he would still wake up, go to the track, and work out with me. His sacrifice and support really enhanced our love, and made me feel pressure to reciprocate his kindness towards me.

The Example of Love Can Heal And Overcome The Fiercest Opponents

I always say that the greatest power in the world is love power. There is no force in heaven and on earth that can defeat love. Never. If you have tried all you know to do and nothing seems to work for you, try love; it is the way to victory. God is love. Whatever situations may arise can be conquered by love. If hate or fear becomes more intense, love more, and with perseverance, all situations submit. For this reason, King Solomon said:

"Place me like a seal over your heart, like a seal on your arm; for love is as strong as death, its jealousy unyielding as the grave. IIt burns like blazing fire, like a mighty flame. Many waters cannot quench love; rivers cannot sweep it away. If one were to give all the wealth of one's house for love, it would be utterly scorned."[9]

Support One Another's Dream

The greatest support I know in the world is moral support. Throwing your full weight behind the pursuit of your spouse is the best you can give them. Did you know you can build a man's confidence if nobody believes in him but you? Even if a person does not believe in themselves but you keep telling the person that you believe him, most times, they will wake up to become somebody, because you believed in them. Affirmations and prophetic declarations are POWERFUL!

Someone's aspirations are their desires yet to be achieved; it is strong desire, longing, hope, and ambition. You must know what your spouse wants to achieve and do with his or her life. Ambition

9   **Songs of Solomon 8:6-7**

is good. Encourage your spouse to have ambition, and see to it that they pursue it. Ambitions that positively affect the lives of others don't birth themselves.

The joy of your spouse must be your everyday pursuit, and whatever your spouse is not satisfied with; you should also be dissatisfied with. Your joy is their joy. Their satisfaction is your satisfaction. You are one.

Be Good Stewards

Stewardship embraces EVERY gift that God has given us. Genesis 1:28 says, "God blessed them and said to them, 'Be fruitful and increase in number; fill the earth and subdue it. Rule over the fish in the sea and the birds in the sky and over every living creature that moves on the ground." Fruitfulness does not only include the fruit of the womb (having babies), but it also includes multiplying everything that God gives you: Connections, ideas, solutions, time, goods, money, talents, wisdom, and so on. In my book, The 12 Undeniable Laws Of Prosperity, I go in much more depth about squeezing the nutrients out of everything that God has given us; this ability is a function of thanksgiving to God. Every person enters your life for a reason. Are you multiplying the impact of that connection for the wellbeing of others? Are you manifesting the ideas that you are given for the benefit of others and the glory of God? Your marriage is a gift. It contains seeds that can multiply into a forest that can transcend culture, language, intellect, economy, denomination, and every other form of division. It is up to you to cherish the seeds that can grow from your marriage enough to sow them. Dr. Myles Munroe said:

"Essentially, being fruitful means releasing our potential. Fruit is an end product. An apple tree may provide cool shade and be beautiful to look at, but until it produces apples it has not fulfilled its ultimate purpose. Apples contain the seeds of future apple trees and, therefore, future apples. However, apples also have something else to offer: a sweet and nourishing food to satisfy human physical hunger. In this sense, fruit has a greater purpose than simply reproducing; fruit exists to bless the world. Every person is born with a seed of greatness. God never tells us to go find seed; it is already within us. Inside each of us is the seed potential for a full forest—a bumper crop of fruit with which to bless the world. We each were endowed at birth with a unique gift, something we were born to do or become that no one else can achieve the way we can. God's purpose is that we bear abundant fruit and release the blessings of our gift and potential to the world."

Summary

- Learn Your Purpose As A Couple

- God Has A Purpose For Your Marriage

- Your Marriage Can Affect The World

- Marriage Is The Foundation Of Creation and The World Society

- Discover Your Purpose As A Couple

- Analyze Where Your Teamwork Works

- Analyze Your Talents and How They Can Be Used To Accent One Another

- Analyze Your Areas Of Increased Wisdom
- Keep Your Marriage As An Example Of Infectious Love
- Love Encourages
- The Senses Pick Up On Infectious Love
- The Example Of Love Can Heal And overcome the fiercest opponents
- Support One Another's Dream
- Know one another's aspirations
- Stay tuned to your spouse's joys and discontentment

Exercise Two

1. Write down your talents and those of your spouse.

2. Write down things that you know a lot about (areas of increased wisdom).

3. Write down 5 reasons why your friends call you rather than calling someone else.

4. Write down 5 reasons why your spouse's friends call them. This will help them to understand their role (from your perspective) in the lives of those that call them.

5. Write how you and your spouse can use your talents to accent one another.

6. Pray, "Father, You know the reason that you fashioned my husband and I the way that you have. Reveal to us how we can live our highest potential and please you. I remove

the veils that may blind us of the entirety of your purpose for us, and I declare that you kingdom will manifest in and thru my marriage right now. Amen"

7. Meditate daily on how you can be of greater impact with the above listed assets.

CHAPTER THREE

WATCH YOUR WORDS

"Communication is the ability to ensure that people understand not only what you say but also what you mean. It is also the ability to listen to and understand others. Developing both of these aspects of communication takes a lot of time, patience, and hard work."

— Myles Munroe, *The Purpose and Power of Love & Marriage*

Encourage the pursuit of your spouse' dream in words, genuine faith, and deeds. Nobody survives in an environment where unkind and derogatory words are spoken. One of the greatest disservices you can do to a person is to destroy their self image with words that demean, reduces and breaks instead of make. You have to encourage each other's pursuits in kind, sincere, genuine and faith-filled words!

The Story of Caleb and His Wife

"Before we got married, I asked you your definition of love. You said that you don't know. I asked you what your vision was, you said, 'none'! You are low on IQ, you have inferiority complex, your knowledge of the word of God is inaccurate. I am everything. You are no one!"

Caleb went to his pastors' office and shoved his phone under his nose and said, "Read Pastor, read. You asked me to love my wife at all cost, whether she is loveable or not. Now, see the text message she sent me last night."

"Brother Caleb," he said, "Would you please let me call your wife to my office, so we could talk about this?" . "Whether or not you call her that is not my concern. I came to tell you that it is over with us, she cannot be married to a low IQ man with no vision and no purpose. I work all day just to keep the home and our two children, and yet my wife is lazy, out doing nothing, and still sending me this kind of text message? I told you she is saucy, loquacious, and foolish. How would a woman who wakes everybody at home with her prayers in the early hours of the morning-speaking in tongues, say this of her husband? She claims to be a Christian, spirit-filled and led, but she is talking to me like this? Pastor, I am tired and I am quitting. I have told you before, but you wouldn't let me, probably because you didn't believe me. Now you have your proof."

The Pastor was able to talk to Caleb and prevail on his wife to come to his office for counsel.

"Pastor, yes I did send the text message. My husband comes home from his office with quarrels, shouting at me, and our kids. He calls me all kinds of derogatory names, abusing me with words, and even sometimes resolves to violence. I have to pay back. My children and I have almost lost our self-esteem because of how much he has wounded us with words"

The Bible says that the universe (seen and unseen) was created with the WORD of God. Then, it goes further to say that the power of life and death lie on our tongues. The power of your words should NOT be taken lightly! If you want circumstances to change in your marriage, it begins with your thoughts, attitudes, and your words expressed towards your spouse.

Name Them According To Their Destiny

Your destinies are tied to your names. Is it any wonder that God would have to change some person's name in the Bible before He could bless? Name your spouse what you want them to be. Names are our identity in the spirit realm. Hence: (1) be careful of destructive names and nicknames and (2) Practice affirmative names and sayings.

If you are saying, "You are lazy", "You are no one", "You are not good enough", and assigning disempowering names to them, this will affect the both of you, and defeat your effort towards a happy marriage. You have to practice assigning names that are consistent with those that God has assigned to them, and you have to do this regardless of what your spouse does. With repetition, the momentum within your home will change. Say things like, "You can do all things with Christ on your side", "You are handsome", "You are a blessing to all who you meet", and if you cannot yet confess these things in truth, begin by blessing your spouse. Declare, "You will be a blessing to everyone you meet", "You will show greater love today and forever more", and when you declare these things, invite Heaven's agreement, and assistance to manifest the change. Do not do this in a way to be offensive. If this is offensive to your spouse, make your declarations in private. Intercessory prayer is very effective in private. It was a practice of Jesus to separate himself as he interceded for the world, so you should also invest time into praying for the advancement of your spouse.

Facilitate "I am" statements

Ensure that "I am" and "you are" is always a part of your home, and when they are used, they are only affirming your God-like-ness. Here are some examples of "I am" statements that you should practice and live on a daily basis. Declare them over your life and that of your spouse and family members.

I am healthy whole and sound.

I am weighing the right weight.

I am an amazing person.

I am healed completely.

I am relieved of aches and pains.

I eat healthy.

I am maintaining a normal blood pressure.

I am beautiful from the inside-out.

I am happy and blessed to have strong bones and teeth according to the word of God.

I am enjoying my beautiful skin in Jesus name.

I am not afraid of natural hormonal changes.

I am well rested; I am not stressed.

I am healed by the stripes of Jesus.

I am whole spiritually, socially, and physically.

I am an energetic being.

I am healthy physically, mentally, emotionally, spiritually, hormonally, relationally, psychologically, socially and corporately.

In turn, you can equally on a daily basis declare these statements into the life of your spouse and children. When you make declarations, you have to know that you are not saying that things are this way now. You are transforming the spiritual and physical atmosphere by declaring that these things be manifested as you vocalize them. You are transforming the vibrations of the atmosphere and universe, and commanding their submission, so that change can be manifested. Remember, God put the Earth in your dominion, so just as a King commands, you must also declare what the state of your environment should be.

Proverbs 22:1 says, "A good name is more desirable than great riches; to be esteemed is better than silver or gold". Riches cannot buy a rich name! A good name is formed simply by repetition of words to volumes of people. Reputation usually is in connection with character, but for short stints, reputation can be inflated in a good or bad way without demonstrations of character. Your responsibility as a spouse is to maintain a good reputation for you and your household; keep a royal remembrance of your family. You can maintain a reputation that encourages and challenges others to strive harder, to achieve godliness, and reach their highest potential in life by speaking positive affirmations and assigning names that increase your spouse.

Avoid Criticism and Contempt

In his book, The Seven Principles That Make A Marriage Work, Dr. John Gottman said that he can tell within the first five minutes of meeting a couple whether or not they were a lifetime marriage or whether they would divorce. When I read his statement,

I was quite astonished, and as I read further, I found that he had done a study monitoring the body's response to words and actions between husbands and wives for 18+ years. Thru his discovery, he said that there are "four horsemen of the apocalypse" that cause horrible consequences to the health and well-being of the body: criticism, contempt, defensiveness, and stonewalling. When the couple uses too many of these types of words, the marriage will not work simply as a means of protecting their health.

These types of words are typically used together; one leading to the other. They cause the body to break out in sweat, the blood pressure changes, the temperature rises, and over long stints of time, the body systems are less effective; making participants susceptible to many illnesses and diseases. Many scientists have studied the effects of our words on our surroundings, but you must also know that your words greatly affect your spouse and your environment.

Avoid destructive criticism and contempt. Hold each other in high esteem with mutual respect. The things that you say become representations of who you say them about. Examples: "You always.....", "You never...", "O! So Mr. doesn't want to follow rules, wants to talk?" such statements and derogatory words should be avoided. To avoid the horrible repercussions that come along with poisonous words, you must know the laws of speaking and listening to your spouse.

As you speak:

- No blaming or no "you" statements
- Talk about how you feel in a specific situation, use "I" statements
- Express a positive need

As you listen:
- Be aware of your partner's enduring vulnerabilities
- Turn toward your partner and postpone your own agenda
- Be tolerant by believing there are always two valid realities
- Make understanding your partner the goal of listening
- Be non-defensive
- Do not respond right away
- Get in touch with the partner's pain.
- Be empathic—summarizing the partner's view and validating by completing a sentence like "I can totally understand why you have these feelings and needs, because...."

Listening and responding to feedback that directly addresses our own imperfections is not easy; neither is it typically practiced until marriage. Using, "I" statements rather than "you" statements greatly cuts back on the other person's perception of attack.

When my husband and I first got married, I was very proficient at seeing and addressing things that I perceived were "wrong". I would say things like, "You always leave the shower head pointing to the bathroom floor!", "You always leave the vegetables in the wrong part of the refrigerator", and so on. In response to my accusation, he would typically respond with one of the other horsemen (criticism, contempt, stonewalling, or defensiveness). A typical response would be, "If you didn't always...", "O! So you want to talk?", or silence as his blood pressure rose and rose as a result of the attack.

In my graduate studies at Liberty University, we had to use Dr. John Gottman's book, The Seven Principles That Make A Marriage

Work as a textbook for one of my classes. As I read this book, I was able to see many of my own influences in the argumentative nature that would invade our space at times. I had to learn how to say words and address my husband in love. Since, I have learned to say, "I really appreciate when you do…", "If you could do…, it would be so helpful", and as a result, the four horsemen do not sneak up on us as commonly.

Be Careful With Volume

When you talk too much, you lose respect, so be careful and constructive with what you say to each other. A few well-articulated thoughts would do more than a million words that hurt. Even more, watch how loud you speak to your spouse. If raising your volume is your only defense, you must turn inward, and examine yourself. Volume typically causes others to perceive hostility, and invites the four horsemen that we spoke of before. If you would like to maintain a happy marriage, you want to cultivate an environment of cooperation rather than conflict. How can you be a better listener and more understanding of your spouse's views? How can you make solutions without becoming loud? You and your spouse should agree on how to effectively listen to one another.

One of the greatest things that you can do to guard you and your spouse's spirits, is to guard your words. Analyze today what your speaking habits are, and how you can change them for the sake of your world-class, happy marriage.

Summary

- Watch Your Words

- Name Your Spouse According To Their Destiny. Examples: You are healthy, wealthy, and wise.

- Be careful of destructive names and nicknames

- Practice affirmative names and sayings

- Facilitate "I am" statements. Ensure that "I am" and "you are" is always a constructive statement.

- Avoid Criticism, Contempt, Defensiveness, and Stonewalling: Examples: "You always.....", "You never...", "O! So Mr. Doesn't Want To Follow Rules Wants To Talk?"

- Be Careful With Volume. It is Better To Go Lower Than Higher

Exercise

Take a 30 day talk test. Get a notebook and write on it, "a 30 day talk test". Number it day one through day thirty. For every day you lose your temper and talk fowl, mark that day * and the day you did not, mark it +. Then repeat this process for a 90 day period and or even beyond until all the * have turned to +.

CHAPTER FOUR

WATCH YOUR PHYSIOLOGY

"The scars from mental cruelty can be as deep and long-lasting as wounds from punches or slaps but are often not as obvious. In fact, even among women who have experienced violence from a partner, half or more report that the man's emotional abuse is what is causing them the greatest harm."

— **Lundy Bancroft,** *Why Does He Do That?: Inside the Minds of Angry and Controlling Men*

Physiology is the scientific study of how people, animals, and plants function. Being aware of your own physiology means that you are mindful of your emotions, your state of being, and you are willing to protect your marriage from negative actions or words by creating a plan. As Dr. Myles Munroe said, "How someone else perceives and understands us depends only 7 percent on what we say, 38 percent on how we say it, and 55 percent on what we are doing when we say it."

The Story Of Albert And Pat

Albert, being sanguine, and a salesman, talks every time and all the time. You cannot stand in his presence without hearing him cracking jokes and shows. He is loud and enjoys being noticed. Even in his sleep, he talks. But Pat, his wife, on the other hand is melancholy and withdraws most of the time. She is given to much thinking rather than to talking. Her job as a banker exasperates her most of the time. She comes home from the office and wants to quickly fix the family meal and retire to bed on time; preparing for another day in the office which is equally going to be tasking.

"I don't understand why my wife will not talk to me when I want to talk. I have been putting up with it, but I can't any longer. I got married so that I would be able to express myself all the time. I can't understand why she does not talk when I want to, and she is always complaining of being tired.

I don't even want to talk about the issue of sex. She wouldn't allow me touch her most of the time; all in the guise of being tired. She says, 'Honey, I am so tired. I must rest so that I can be fit for work the next day.' I am not married to a log of wood, or a dead tree. She must talk to me because that's what I want."

Appropriate Timing

The most important message in the world can be mistaken if the timing is not right. Sweating, blood pressure, pulse, temperature, feelings, sleep deprivation, and emotions are all signs of bodily stress. Any conversation that does not relieve physiological symptoms has a chance at being futile if introduced when the person's body is already demonstrating signs of stress.

I know when my husband is tired, if he has just gotten out of traffic, received bad news, or hungry, I recognize the physiological symptoms, and allow him a break. At times, I still desire his companionship, but I know that it is for the interest of our happy, peaceful home that I choose another time to converse with him. When the physiological symptoms are apparent, the best things that I can do to spend time is to assist in relaxing him regardless of my wants or needs.

Keep Secrets

In the event that your spouse divulges information to you, you should keep these conversations between the two of you. If the conversation had the power to sway his or her body functions, this conversation is probably still marinating their spirits with lessons, and may cause the feeling of betrayal if you share the content. You should learn to keep feedback, errors, and accidents as sacred. Do not blast them to the world. Your spouse will not feel safe and secure if you demonstrate a pattern of telling the world of their most vulnerable expressions. When there are concerns to be addressed as there would always be, let it be addressed in a private place.

Do Not Act On Exterior But Interior

Think before you act. Avoid surface emotional responses. Act on purpose. Watch your own body functions. Notice, are your hands sweating? Can you feel the blood pulsing thru your veins? Is your heart rate faster than normal? Are you tired or hungry? Is your temperature okay? Is your heart and mind at peace? If you know that you are demonstrating symptoms of stress, make an internal decision to hold your tongue until you can speak words of love in a way that will not stimulate the other's perception of attack. Transform the momentum of your thoughts by reminding yourself of the good in the situation or in the past, remind yourself of your love, and advocate for your love to grow more intense; rather than allowing your emotions or a circumstance to conquer.

Know When Your Spouse Needs Intimacy

The sexual organs respond to stimulation. When the sexual organs respond, but are not recognized, it traps hormones that are supposed to be released. It can alter confidence, future interest, and it can stimulate conflict.

When a woman is aroused, her nipples begin to rise, the temperature escalates, the color of the nipples darken, the lips and the vagina becomes lubricated. When a man is aroused, the penis hardens and the temperature rises.

When your spouse desires intimacy, you can be playful with charm to excite the both of you about intimacy. If either of you have unforgiveness, it really dampens the enjoyment of intimacy so you must dissolve frictional topics and forgive to have maximum stimulation in sex. Enjoy sex!

Summary

- Watch Your Physiology

- Appropriate Timing

- Sweating, Blood pressure, pulse, temperature, feelings, emotions are signs of bodily stress. Allow physiology to regulate before engaging in stimuli conversations.

- Keep feedback, errors, and accidents as sacred. Do not blast them to the world. Address concerns in a private place.

- Do Not Act On Exterior But Interior: Avoid Emotional Responses

Exercise

Write goals for the month. How much time have you spent doing what your spouse would like to do? Make it a goal this month to invest more time doing what your spouse would like to do. Add this on your schedule and specify at what point in the day you actually plan to spend this time with your spouse. Be very specific, measurable, attainable, realistic, and timely with your goals.

CHAPTER FIVE

KEEP FIRM BOUNDARIES

"Boundaries define us. They define what is me and what is not me. A boundary shows me where I end and someone else begins, leading me to a sense of ownership. Knowing what I am to own and take responsibility for gives me freedom. Taking responsibility for my life opens up many different options. Boundaries help us keep the good in and the bad out. Setting boundaries inevitably involves taking responsibility for your choices. You are the one who makes them. You are the one who must live with their consequences. And you are the one who may be keeping yourself from making the choices you could be happy with. We must own our own thoughts and clarify distorted thinking."

— **Henry Cloud,** *Boundaries: When to Say Yes, How to Say No, to Take Control of Your Life*

When God transferred Israel to new locations, the first things that he would tell them was their boundaries. He would say, "From the Jordan River down to the…". The boundaries for settlement were very specific, and you should also demonstrate specific boundaries within your territories. You must have specific boundaries for your time, finances, property, affection, your body, and all other things that are your territories. Certain boundaries should be designated only for your spouse to explore. If you don't understand certain boundaries in your marriage, you would abuse the sanctity of that holy convocation.

So I want to point to you some areas of your marriage that you need to keep with all diligence.

The Story of Pastor Amos and Marilyn

Bang, bang, a hard knock, on the door of Pastor Amos's living room. "On Saturday evening? I should be resting, meditating on the Scriptures, and preparing for Sunday service," he muttered. He opened the door only to find Marilyn standing by his door in tears. "Come in Mari," he demanded." What is the matter? Why are you crying?"

"My husband," she said. "Your husband! What about him," he queried. "I came in from choir practice this evening only to meet my mother-in-law in the house". "Your mother-in-law? And were you not aware that she was coming?" he asked. "Not at all!" she said. "And you need to know why she came?" His face started to turn as he stood and stared full of unanswered questions. "Why?" he asked.

"My mother-in-law came because my husband told her everything that is happening in our home, down to our bedroom. Did you know that my mother-in-law knows about all the men I dated before I married her son? Did you that she knows the last time my husband and I had sexual intercourse? Did you know that she practically knows my husband's salary and all his projects? Did you know that there is nothing that I have told my husband about me that my mother-in-law does not know? Now, she said she needs a third and a fourth child. And that if I don't give her a third and a fourth child, she would find another wife for her son."

The most annoying part of all is that she told me all this in the presence of our kids-Joy and David, and my husband does not see anything wrong with any of this."

Marriage Conversations

In his book, The Purpose and Power of Love & Marriage, Dr. Myles Munroe said:

"Once a man and woman have married, the only thing they should receive from their parents is advice and counsel, and then only when they ask for it. Parents should not offer opinions or advice without being asked. To do so undermines the development of the leadership and self-determination of the couple. When they married, the leadership and decision-making responsibilities transferred from their former homes to the new home they are building together. All leadership now devolves on them. They are responsible for making their own decisions. Part of cultivating companionship is learning how to exercise these responsibilities effectively together."

Some conversations are intended to be maintained as marriage conversations. You must have boundaries, and you must work at keeping all marriage conversations behind closed doors! Men talk to their wives differently in the secret of their bedroom than they would outside the bedroom. The bedroom is the holy of holies of the married couple, and as the holy of holies of the tabernacle and temple of Moses and Solomon are never to be seen but kept secret, that is how all marriage conversations should be kept secret. There are some words that no other ear in the world must hear with the exception of you and your spouse. The boundaries should be drawn from the Bible and from agreement with your spouse.

Keep Secrets

When your spouse may divulge very tender and emotional information when physiological symptoms are apparent. In tears, in fright, in rage, or in disappointment, you can be privy to some of your spouse's' greatest vulnerabilities. In the event that your spouse divulges information to you, you should keep these conversations between the two of you. If the conversation had the power to sway his or her body functions, this conversation is probably still marinating their spirits with lessons, and may cause the feeling of betrayal if you share the content. You should learn to keep feedback, errors, and accidents as sacred. Do not blast them to the world. Your spouse will not feel safe and secure if you demonstrate a pattern of telling the world of their most vulnerable expressions. When there are concerns to be addressed as there would always be, let it be addressed in a private place.

Others should not know about your marriage bed

The marriage bed is your holy of holies and it should be kept and treated that way. In the Old Testament, the holy of holies was the ONLY place where the Spirit of God would reign and linger. The priests were appointed by God to enter, only on certain days, and never empty handed (they always had to sacrifice something). Additionally, they had to wear certain attire and cleanse themselves in a directed way before they could enter. The marriage bed is the holy of holies for you and your spouse. You should have specific boundary lines and requirements to enter it. Allow your bedroom to be the sanctuary, the secret place where you increase your love. Marriage is honorable among all, and the bed undefiled; but fornicators and adulterers God will judge[10].

---

10 Hebrews 13:4

Do not disagree before children

Children learn better by observation than by mere words. They do what you do more than what you say. When you disagree in their presence, they learn how to treat you (as their parents), and they learn how to treat others. If you talk over each other; rather than listening, and understanding, they will emulate the behavior that they see. Your home impacts your generations (beyond your first) and the generations of others, so be careful.

Consult one another about situations of family impact (financial, spiritual, business and any others)

The day you got married, was the day that you stopped being independent. Whatever the decisions, ventures you want to undertake, you would have to consult with each other before going ahead. It is a family; a team. Matters that border on finances, the spiritual well being and business life of the family must be agreed on by both parties before any action is taken. Despite what your society, culture, or your ego tells you, if you are married, the Bible says that the two become one. Therefore, matters that you used to entertain and solve alone, now become matters that you both must settle together.

Align Your Values with Your Time

Values are principles or standards of behavior. The world is made to run on certain principles or laws as you know but these laws are aligned with time. For instance there is a natural law established by God that every 365 (sometimes 66) days the earth will revolve around the sun completely; this is the basis for our calendar and makes up one year.

Don't waste time; align your time with your values! You decide what is important to you versus what is not important to you. If you desire a happy marriage, you must commit to the continual investment of dedicated time.

Good diamonds are known by their condition: they are closely analyzed with microscopes, they are clear without discoloration, and they do not have scratches. The most quality diamonds have greater weight, they sparkle and shine, they have little to no scratches, they are clear, and a diamond expert has declared a grade based on their condition. They are insured and protected; most being placed in a vault, or a locked and recorded space

Time works similar to diamonds. The most valuable time is un-adulterated; it is free from thoughts of work, comparisons, and other obligations. It has been closely analyzed and protected to ensure that it is of maximum quality to the recipient. You must sanctify valuable time for your spouse and protect it as a jeweler would do for his most prized diamonds.

Make Your Spouse a Clear Priority through Your Schedule

Fidelity is any breach of sanctified marriage assets. Time, property, connections, wisdom, information, solutions, or anything else that you and your spouse cherish as a couple. When any of these assets are shared with another person, place, or thing, the betrayal feels similarly. Who and what is top of the list in your daily schedule? Your job or time with your spouse? Your spouse is just as important as your arm, your leg, your mouth, or your nose. He or she has become a part of your being. Though this connection may not be seen outside of the marriage bed, the connection is very clear in the Spirit. Your spouse should maintain the same priority as you hold to your own well-being. If you shower, you should also be concerned that your spouse do the same. If you eat, you should also be concerned that your spouse do the same. Yes, they are grown, but they have now joined with you as one being. Therefore, they should be a clear priority on your schedule; second only to God, and equal to your own well-being.

Do not allow ANYTHING to intrude on making your marriage a priority

Your marriage is your primary responsibility (after God), so do not allow obligations (school, work, parenting, family) to interfere with the marriage priority. What you do with your marriage, you will be accountable for when you stand before God for judgement. Put first things first. Keep Your Marriage As 2nd Priority After God. The place of God must not be replaced with marriage and the place of marriage must not be replaced with something else. The three stranded cord means that you become one with God and your spouse; no one else: not your children, not your family, not your job[11]. Is that clear enough?

Summary

- Keep Firm Boundaries
- Keep marriage conversations behind closed doors
- Others should not know about your marriage bed
- Do not disagree before children
- Consult one another about situations of family impact (financial, spiritual, business, etc.)

---

11   Ecclesiastes 4:9-12

- Align Your Values With Your Time
- Make Your Spouse A Clear Priority Thru Your Schedule
- Do not allow ANYTHING to intrude on making your marriage a priority (obligations, school, work, parenting, family)
- Keep Your Marriage As 2nd Priority After God
- 3 stranded chord means that you become one with God and your spouse; no one else: not your children, not your family, not your job.

Exercise

Decide today, write it down in your notepad, and mark it in your calendar, that you would resolve your marital issues within yourselves. No more will you reveal your marriage problems to people who do not have the ability to make it better. The word of God and practical wisdom has all the answers to your marriage challenge. Go for it. Never again should you expose your spouse to the world.

CHAPTER SIX

CONTROL YOUR INTAKE

"I will not let anyone walk through my mind with
their dirty feet."

— Mahatma Gandhi

"You are what you eat." I suppose you have heard that
statement over and over again. How true! And this
does not only apply to food intake but also to life in
general.

The Story Of Mrs. Donald

I don't understand why my husband will go and be hanging
out with the "lows" of the neighborhood. Imagine that my husband
will go sit with people who are going nowhere and coming
from nowhere. If he doesn't have anything to do, can't he just sit at
home and study God's word? Mrs. Donald complained.

My husband wakes up in the morning, instead of taking the
time to pray and study God's word; the first thing he flips on
is the television. How can a man just wake up in the morning
and start out with the television? I don't understand it. What's he
teaching our kids? What kind of foundation is he laying for the
family? Even though he has no paid employment right now, can't
he just stay and develop himself? Why can't he call the family to
pray together in the morning and in the night before we retire to

bed. I tried to lead the family in daily morning devotion, he keeps frustrating it.

The books we bought before we married that we agreed we were going to read together, he never reads them. Instead, he goes hanging around with people I don't understand. I can't take it anymore. I keep a paid job to keep the home and yet he frustrates me by his responsibilities. I am tired and quibbled.

Be Careful Of Your Intake

An old saying is, "What you put in comes out!" Whether that means food, music, comments, videos, or whatever it may be; if you put it in, it will come out, so you must be very careful of your intake. Guard your Spirit because when it becomes contaminated, you lose the ability to see and discern God. God requires a clean vessel to reside, so you must choose to maintain your cleanliness by controlling your intake, and discarding of those things that are not nutrients to your spirit and your marriage.

Media

You emulate what you see. The media is a great tool in the hand of God and of Satan for good and for bad. What do you feed your mind and spirit from the television, radio and newspapers?

Media exposure subliminally reprograms the mind, and due to the content being interpreted at such a voracious speed, it is very difficult to captivate each thought and address whether each is one that you want to add into your most sacred tool of creation: your imagination. As you are feeding your mind thru media exposure, you are comparing with previous programming of the mind, you are deciding whether you like what you see now better, and you are even programming actions steps within your mind for future encounters with experiences that you have watched.

I have seen people who invest a lot of time into following the news, and become very worrisome because the news typically isolates its focus on the bad things going on in the world rather than the good. People who do not take time to sift what they see correlate presumptions of the world, and are reprogrammed by fictitious unbiblical infestations of the mind. Additionally, if something like porn is taken in, the viewer becomes less sensitive to the tenderness of their spouse in the marriage bed. They draw comparisons between their spouse's bodies and choice positions, they input new desired activities, and they even presume the same outcome (whether it be screaming, sensation, level of enjoyment, etc.). Pornography is an attack of the Kingdom of Darkness and typically welcomes itself in when the couple is vulnerable, and to get it out, it requires intense prayer, and reprogramming of the mind to regain sensitivity to the appeal of his or her spouse.

Music

If there is anything that I know that has far-reaching influence among tribes and people, it is music. No wonder Satan seeks to control the music industry of all nations. And you know that closely related with music is drugs, so watch it. Don't just listen to music; find out first the spirit behind it before you listen to it. Every music artist leaves his or her spirit in their music. Music is spirit; it communicates the spirit of the singer. If an artist is dirty, his music will communicate and dump dirtiness on all those who listen to it. Be careful not to contaminate your spirit. These contaminations can have a great negative effect on your marriage. It can degrade your perceptions on the value of your marriage, your spouse's circumstances, or even your spouse. Alternatively, music about love, that encourages loving behavior can also stimulate you to behave in a loving way before your spouse.

Environment

It matters where you live, work and play. Lot lived in Sodom and Gomorrah and the Scripture says that his righteous soul was tormented and vexed by their lawless deeds.[12] You cannot keep being righteous and truthful to God, if you work, live and stay at certain places. Flee every appearance of evil.[13] Stay around people and places that encourage your marriage. If they stir division, create negative thoughts on marriage, or disgrace your reputation; flee!

Summary

Control your intake from:
- Relationships
- Media
- Music
- Environment

Exercise

Sit down with your spouse for seven days in a row and write down your intake. What music have you both listened to? What

---

12   2 Peter 2: 6-8
13   1 Thess. 5:22

televisions shows have you watched? What observations have marinated in your mind? Who has advised you this week (good or bad)? What is the outcome of your intake? How has it affected your mood, your thoughts, your attitudes, your words? Decide whether you think that your intake has had a good or bad influence on your marriage, and how you can make it better.

CHAPTER SEVEN

COMPETE WITH DEMONSTRATIONS OF LOVE

"Satisfied needs produce fulfilled people, and fulfilled people are free to pursue and exercise their full potential as human beings. The primary goal, then, in any relationship should be the meeting of needs. We should not concentrate so much on meeting our own needs, but those of the other person in the relationship. A good test for the health of a relationship is to ask ourselves periodically whose needs we are meeting, ours or theirs? If we are focusing on our needs, the relationship is in trouble. In successful, healthy relationships, both parties put a priority on meeting the needs of the other."

— Myles Munroe, *The Purpose and Power of Love & Marriage*

When you come into a marriage for what you will gain, you will lose; all you have would be frustration and disappointment. Come into marriage with the idea of out-doing your mate. I call it love competition. When you are not just waiting for your spouse to give, but ready to out-do every of his or her actions, then you are ready for a vibrant, good flavored marriage. See, love out-does one another in good deeds.

The Story of Mr. Williams, Raymond, and Esther

Esther is the last child of her family, "daddy's baby" of the home. As far as she is concerned, being the baby of the family, everyone must give to her, and that was the case in her family.

Every festive period is another time to increase her wardrobe. Every other school semester was another opportunity to increase her savings, from daddy, mommy and all of her six older siblings. They know that Esther has to go to school and that Esther must wear a new dress for another Christmas; always at the receiving end. Her birthday was a family and societal birthday as family and friends will come march and celebrate with the last born of the Williams.

Her father was influential in the society and being "daddy's baby", you could hardly see daddy without Esther. In functions and ceremonies, it is Esther and Mr. Williams.

Her mind has been set in a cast to believe that she must always be receiving, everybody owes her something. It was with this mindset that Esther met and married Raymond.

Raymond, being a believer, understands the place of giving, but he feels that in spite of all that he is doing, Esther never reciprocates. Esther's birthday is a feast, and Raymond has never failed to live to her expectation. Raymond has never received anything from Esther; even on his birthday. Raymond feels that he has endured 3 years of this frustration; not being appreciated and celebrated by his wife. Now, he has decided to vent his frustration and disappointment through verbal assault, he has had enough.

Life is about giving and receiving

God designed every living thing to be born of a seed. Love, virtue, joy, peace, and wisdom are living things. They require seeds sown to have a presence. If you desire to grow these things in your marriage, you must initiate the growth regardless of the actions that you see from your spouse or your surroundings. The following are some ways to flavor your marriage with demonstrations of love.

Ask yourself, "How can I show him/her love more than he/she shows me? How can I show more love than I ever have before? When you have truly answered that question and are mindful of it, then you are in for the real treat. This is not something you think of once in a while, but a vibrant, everyday living reality of your marriage.

Keep records of right

Example: My husband woke up and gave me a kiss, my wife made me breakfast, etc. love does not keep record of wrong, but rather, keeps record of right. You are not married to a perfect person, but there are things that your spouse has done that are truly exemplary, celebrate those actions, always remind him or her of those things. What you give attention to and celebrate grows. Intentionally outweigh the bad in your thoughts, in your words, and in your actions. The Bible says that we should not be overcome by evil but that we should overcome evil with good.[14] .When you don't give expression to those grudges of yours; they will die a natural death.

---

14 **Romans 12:21**

Show Honor

To honor someone means to treat them or regard them with special attention and respect. Treat your spouse with dignity, special attention and respect. He is your king. She is your queen. Give him or her special attention. Always show excitement when you see your spouse. Speak of them as you would a King or Queen; not dependent on your feelings or circumstance, but on their role and your decision to spend your life with them.

Can you tell me the last time you saw your spouse and you were full of excitement and the deep feeling of love and romance as you had when you were still courting and dating? You can rekindle it.

Treat them as royalty

There is a common saying, "If the owner of a thing calls it trash, the person that does not own it, will use it as garbage dump." It simply means that the value you place on what you have is the same value that others will place on it. The day you start insulting yourself, others will join you.

He is your king. She is your queen. Treat them as such. You cannot bow down and revere government authorities or scream and chant for sports players, and you don't do the same to your spouse. What you cannot give your spouse; don't give it to any other person. To you, your spouse should be the most revered person on Earth because they are an extension of you. Make them distinguishable in your words and actions; set them above the world. Have you not read in the Scriptures how Sarah calls

Abraham her Lord?[15]. Who do you resemble? Be like your mother, Sarah, that bore you.

Always Increase Your Charm

Aside from love and affection, charm is what initiates and sustains attraction. Charm is the actions unspoken: the twinkle in the eye before the kiss, the wink, the playful laugh. Charm can be an intimate dance or song; any notion that says, "I adore you now and forever". It is the body language that is widely broadcasted on television and used largely to entice people into premarital and extramarital affairs, but many marriages lack charm.

Marriage is a place where charm can be completely free and unleashed because eros love embraces the erotic aspect of charm. You have full permission in Heaven and Earth to stimulate EVERY fiber of your spouse's being, so why wait? Experiment. Learn how you can stimulate their memories, their seven senses (taste, touch, smell, hearing, sight, proprioception, and vestibular), and send messages up their spinal cord and thru every transmitter in their body saying, "I cannot get enough!". Overwhelm your spouse's thoughts with love by elating every part of their being.

The Bible speaks of the preparation that a woman would go thru to transform herself in preparation to be a concubine of the King in Esther 2:12-14:

Before a young woman's turn came to go in to King Xerxes, she had to complete twelve months of beauty treatments prescribed for the women, six months with oil of myrrh and six with perfumes and cosmetics. And this is how she would go to the king:

---

15   2 Peter 3:6

Anything she wanted was given her to take with her from the harem to the king's palace. In the evening she would go there and in the morning return to another part of the harem to the care of Shaashgaz, the king's eunuch who was in charge of the concubines. She would not return to the king unless he was pleased with her and summoned her by name.

She was prepared for ONE WHOLE YEAR to elate the king, and even afterwards, he may not choose her. Your spouse has chosen you to spend the rest of their life! Prepare to elate them! The concubines of King Xerxes strongly elated every sense. Twelve months of beauty treatments caused the skin and body to transform; bringing them to the plumpest and most adored textures, their strongest aroma, their most appealing glow, a baffling figure, and their most poised stature. Treat your spouse as royalty, prepare yourself for them, and stay prepared for them! Do not take rejection personally if your charm seems unfamiliar. Persist in charm. Change the aura of your marriage. Enjoy the freedom of marriage where you have permission to elate a person from head to toe!

Charm is what you wear, your posture, your grooming, and your aura. Charm magnetizes others to you and lets onlookers have high esteem for who you are. It is monogamous and escalates your perceived net worth along with the value of your spouse.

Charm bleeds thru all of the senses by igniting the nose with perfume, the eyes with confident posture, the ears with honey-like, sweet speech, and the touch with choice materials and lotions that make your spouse energetic about touching you again. In order for you to maintain and enrich your charm, you must be conscious of things that ignite their senses that send unspoken messages. What aroma can you wear that would ignite the passions of your spouse? How can you maintain a posture of confidence? Are there disappointments in your life that may have saturated your joy; causing your posture to change? What words can you say that would stimulate a more passionate sexual experience? What can you cook that would stimulate passion? Can you spritz yourself with a flavor that would make you as delightful as their favorite dessert? What materials command your spouse's repeated touch? How can you wear those materials to interest them in touching you? Can you treat your body differently to attract your spouse's touch?

Charm In The Words

Practice affirmative words. A charming person may attract by the unspoken words, but they sustain the attraction by the intellect, wisdom, and sophistication of their speech. Every person measures sophistication differently, but you know the level of speech that attracted your spouse. You know how descriptive you were about the way that they looked and the deeds that they did, and how effective those words were at attracting them back to spend time with you. Charming words are those words that will magnetize them back to you.

I use charming words to attract my husband. Sometimes, I say things like, "Honey. I cannot wait for you to get back home!", "I have something special waiting for you when you get home", "You look handsome when you do...", or, "There is nothing in the world that compares to you". In the Songs of Solomon, many charming words are exchanged between Solomon and the Shunammite woman. This passage has been used for centuries to increase charm. Replace the images and names as you repeat the

"He" and "She" portions of this scripture for powerful charm to manifest in your marriage. Associate yourself and your spouse to this passage. Repeat the scripture as you gaze into your spouse's eyes with charming passion.

"Let him kiss me with the kisses of his mouth— for your love is more delightful than wine. Pleasing is the fragrance of your perfumes; your name is like perfume poured out. No wonder the young women love you! Take me away with you—let us hurry! Let the king bring me into his chambers.

Friends

We rejoice and delight in you; we will praise your love more than wine.

She

How right they are to adore you! Dark am I, yet lovely, daughters of Jerusalem, dark like the tents of Kedar, like the tent curtains of Solomon. Do not stare at me because I am dark, because I am darkened by the sun. My mother's sons were angry with me and made me take care of the vineyards; my own vineyard I had to neglect. Tell me, you whom I love, where you graze your flock and where you rest your sheep at midday. Why should I be like a veiled woman beside the flocks of your friends?

Friends

If you do not know, most beautiful of women, follow the tracks of the sheep and graze your young goats by the tents of the shepherds.

He

I liken you, my darling, to a mare among Pharaoh's chariot horses. Your cheeks are beautiful with earrings, your neck with strings of jewels. We will make you earrings of gold, studded with silver.

She

While the king was at his table, my perfume spread its fragrance. My beloved is to me a sachet of myrrh resting between my breasts. My beloved is to me a cluster of henna blossoms from the vineyards of En Gedi.

He

How beautiful you are, my darling! Oh, how beautiful! Your eyes are doves.

She

How handsome you are, my beloved! Oh, how charming! And our bed is verdant.[16]

The Effect Of Charm

Charming words are words that increase esteem, they reveal the unique attributes that you see in your spouse that separate them from the remainder of the world. Charm acts as a hitch that keeps your spouse returning for more love, intimacy, and affirmation.

Charm alters the thoughts and can be used to manipulate. Charm should not be used to disarm your spouse or deny them

---

16 **Songs of Solomon 1:1-16**

control of their life. Charm should only be used to increase your marriage passion and love rather than to empty wallets and purses from their goals, plans, dreams, or purposes.

Charm has an effect on friends, family, and those who see your love. It causes others to encourage your love because they enjoy seeing the glow of the couple as their posture and stature changes reflecting their intimate needs being addressed.

Charm is not blunt, but is full of surprises. For example, a charming person may sometimes go to bed clothed and some-times unclothed to mix up the appeal and speak messages of sur-prise. Sometimes they may bake a cake just to celebrate your love. Sometimes they may spritz themselves with something sweet to the taste to experiment in the bedroom. Charm is aggressive in its recollection in the mind, and can create a love addiction. People love to see the tactful charm of passionate couples. Different shoes and clothing does affect how we feel about ourselves. We each are embedded with visions for our lives, and when we wear attire that belittles the vision (regardless of whether it was on sale or cheap), it disappoints us, and changes our demeanor. Assess your attire. Decide if you can wear a special attire that may be more stimulating to you and your spouse and increase your charm. Be-gin speaking positive scriptural affirmations that transform your confidence about yourself, so that you can walk upright, relieved of negative thoughts towards yourself, and absent of worries that may negatively affect your posture.

Charm In The Smell

The sense of smell is a powerful tool! It can be used to mag-netize or repel. Look at the skunk. A powerful message is sent thru him; he repels all who see him because they know of his horrendous smell. Look at how people respond if a public restroom is used to poop. People are ashamed for the person that used the bathroom in such a way, and they will not use it after them. The opposite response is also true. Look at the rose. Billions of dollars are spent annually just on the scent of the rose: perfumes contain it, clipped roses are given as gifts on multiple holidays, and they are one of the most commonly planted flowers simply because of their delightful smell. You want more appeal and charm than the rose. It is not requesting perversion or flirtatious behavior, but it commands attention, and awe. Try scents that can ignite the interest and magnetize your spouse.

Charm in the Taste

Apple pie, red velvet cake, carrots, celery, meatloaf; these all have different taste sensations. Your spouse has foods that are delightful to their tastes. They have sprays that are delightful to their tastes. Be playful in the kitchen and everywhere you go. Ignite the taste on as many occasions as possible. Mix vegetable glycerin (to give a sweet taste and soft feel) and water, spray, and play with the mixture in your lovemaking. Have fun stimulating the taste in your love!

Charm in the Touch

Cottons, velvet, satins, and polyesters all have a different sensation to the touch. Dry skin, bumpy skin, moist skin, and healthy skin all have a different sensations to the touch. Jiggly skin, tight skin, loose skin, plum skin all has a different sensation to the touch. You must learn what your spouse likes to feel. When they receive a feeling to their touch that stimulates their senses, it will magnetize them for more; it will not leave their thoughts even in your absence. Their mind will wander into how charming you are: how you smelled, looked, felt, and tasted.

Stimulate the senses and maintain strong unspoken messages of love, want, attraction, and oneness. Say thru your eyes, "I want you and I can't get enough of you!", and never change your message. Be consistent in your charm. Regardless of what changes in your marriage: if your spouse makes a good decision, bad decision, they disappoint you, they lie, and whatever else could go wrong, commit to your charm. Speak with your body language. Commit to the message that I love you and I want you thru good and bad. Meditate and repeat the below affirmations (scriptural and unscriptural) to increase your charm:

"I am a magnet for my husband/wife and my husband/wife is a magnet for me. He/she is elating every one of my senses now. His/her love is overwhelming to my memory and my senses. I am desiring him/her with every fiber of my being now and I will for the rest of my life."

"God is filling me with abundant charm that will attract my spouse to me now and forevermore!"

Summary

- Compete With Demonstrations Of Love
- Ask yourself, "How can I show him/her love more than he/she shows me?
- Keep records of right. Example: My husband woke up and gave me a kiss, my wife made me breakfast, etc.

- Intentionally outweigh the bad in your thoughts, in your words, and in your actions
- Show Honor
- Always show excitement to see your spouse
- Speak of them as you would a King or Queen (not dependent on your feelings but on their role and your decision to spend your life with them)
- Others will treat them based on how you treat them
- Treat them as royalty
- Make them distinguished in your words and actions; set them above the world
- Always increase your charm
- Charm every sense

Exercise

Go get a gift that befits your spouse right now and with all honor even if it means to kneel down before them, present the gift to them. Surprise them. Tell them that you just want to appreciate them. That you are thankful and grateful to God for giving them to you, and for all the love, care and protection you have enjoyed with them in the years of your marriage.

CHAPTER EIGHT

SET GOALS

"If you want to live a happy life, tie it to a goal, not to people or things."

— Albert Einstein

What are goals? Goals are specific and measurable steps to achieve a vision. They are vision with feet and are always measured with time. Couples cannot afford to leave their lives to chance.

Wise and visionary spouses don't leave their lives to chance, but always set goals, and develop plans to achieve those goals. Your goal might be: "I want to spend 2 hours per day undivided with my spouse", "I want to spend 1 hour daily showing affection before sex", "I want a date night with my spouse per week", "I want to pray together with my spouse daily for 30 min", I want to spend 1 hour per day doing acts of service", "I want to give 100 compliments on physical appearance and business success every-day", "I want to make my spouse breakfast daily."

The Story Of Samuel and Belinda

Samuel is a goal-setter. At the age of 5, he said, "Mommy, I want to learn how to read before I turn six." At seven years of age, he said, "I will learn my multiplication and division tables before I turn eight. At age 18, Samuel said, "I want to go to college and graduate as an engineer; Summa Cum Laude from my

University"; he did as he said. As a result of his goals, he always surpassed his academic standards and what was expected from him at his age and grade.

When Samuel was 24, he started to think about getting married. He had completed engineering school and innovative revolutionary designs that generated him millions of dollars in royalties. He wanted a woman that can increase his current status, so he wrote down a letter to God that said:

"Dear Almighty God,

Your Word says that you do not want man to be alone. I have not found a suitable helpmate for myself, and I desire to find her before I turn 27 years of age. I want a woman who is slim because I want to do a lot of traveling and leading people (young and old). I want her to be able to keep up with a fast-paced life, so I want her to be of healthy stature. I want her to dress as a business woman with business suits and royal attire. I want her to be shorter than I am and near my complexion. I want her breasts to be full enough to feed my children, but not too full to hurt her back. I want her physical stature to be hypnotizing and alluring to me. I want her to be a woman of God and a leader in our spiritual and business life. I want her to be intellectual and sophisticated; able to lead all of my business affairs in my absence. God, your word says that if I am obedient to your commands that you will give me the desires of my heart. I thank you because I can see this woman, and I know that you have consecrated her for me. I break any chords that may separate her from me now, and I remove unforgiveness from the both of our hearts and heads. I erase any contracts that Satan may have signed to hinder her and I from our meeting, and relinquish us from hindrances by the blood of Jesus. I yield myself to the development that you need to do in me to be prepared for my bride. I release your angels to endow her with the wisdom, virtues, and support that she needs to prepare for our marriage. I release the blessing of Abraham and Sarah, Boaz and Ruth (the blessing that livened their marriages) on my wife and I right now. May your Kingdom come in my life now. Amen."

When Samuel was 26 years of age and a largely successful engineer, he met the woman of his dreams, Belinda. The letter that he had written to God sat under his pillow for two years, and she fit the description precisely. They began setting weekly, monthly, and yearly goals in their marriage, and their love was infectious and intoxicating.

The Importance Of Goal-Setting

When there are no set goals, there will be nothing in particular to pursue; no challenge and no purposeful pursuit. Without goals, there will be no motivation whatsoever to achieve, no motivation, and life becomes floppy and a drag. Your execution and manifestation is brought to fruition by the goals or targets you set for yourself. God gives the idea, the dream, or the visions, and we manifest it on the Earth. Marriage goals are milestones that you can achieve to attain a greater marriage.

How To Make Goals For Manifestation

Goal setting is a wisdom key that enhances achievements. There is an acronym that specifies the method at which we create goals; it is called the SMART method. That means that the goals you have set must be:

Specific: There is no vagueness in goal setting. What do you want to achieve? State it in clear terms.

Measurable: How would you measure a goal. If you want to love your spouse more, you have to say, how you will demonstrate that love. Will you spend one hour undivided with them? Will you answer the phones one day per week for his business? Answer! Actions! Walk your talk.

Attainable: Your goals must be something within reach though you have not yet manifested it. Don't be afraid to dream big but just be sure it is something you can achieve. Attainable goals are those that you can comprehend a strategy to manifest.

Realistic: Don't make unrealistic goals. Be real. You know what you can and cannot do.

Timely: One of the best ways to measure goals is time and money. Set daily goals, weekly goals, monthly goals and even annual goals. What can you do to serve your spouse this week? Examples: "I will fix her dinner for the whole week." or "I will set aside $150.00 when I get my royalty check to buy him some new dress shirts". After you have formulated the goal, you give expression to it and follow through on it to completion.

Be about your word enough to walk your talk. You said that you want to have a happy marriage, right? Invest! It's not weakness to serve your spouse. Do it.

Summary

- Set Goals - *Examples: "I want to spend 2 hours per day undivided with my spouse", "I want to spend 1 hour daily showing affection before sex", "I want a date night with my spouse 1 per week", "I want to pray together daily for 30 min", I want to spend 1 hour per day doing acts of service", "I want to give 100 compliments on physical appearance and business success everyday", "I want to make my spouse breakfast daily".*

- What can you do to serve your spouse?

- Make goals to increase your love (weekly, monthly, yearly)

- SMART (specific, measurable, attainable, realistic, timely) goals

Exercise

Get a notepad and title it "My Goal Note Book." In it, write down 21 things you want to achieve this year. Make the goals weekly, monthly, quarterly and annually. Set deadlines for all of them. Set your first month goals to increase your marriage. Write SMART goals that plant seeds of love in your marriage. Do you need to transform your sex life? What is hindering it from being enjoyable? Are you tired or angry? How can you rearrange your day to ensure that you are in full throttle for your spouse? Do you need to date more? How can you make this possible? What are your spouse's desires of you? How can you make time to meet their desires? Set goals for your spiritual life, your finances, your business, set some for your children, and see to it that you check on that note every week to see how far you have gone and how much is yet to be done.

CHAPTER NINE

DROP THE CONDITIONS

"The only way love can last a lifetime is if it's unconditional. The truth is this: love is not determined by the one being loved but rather by the one choosing to love."

— Stephen Kendrick, *The Love Dare*

"I cannot love him if he does not apologize" "I cannot love him if he eats my leftover food and leaves me none", "I cannot love her if he raises his voice", "I cannot love her if she doesn't cook", I cannot love him if he doesn't cut the grass." Stop it!

What if God cannot love you unless…? How many times has God given you conditions before He blesses or forgives you?

The Story Of John and His Wife

The husband of a 24 year old mother of 2 came running to Elijah's office to have him intervene in the case between him and his wife. He was a wise man and had very strong compassion towards married couples. Elijah was keen to know what the case was. The lady was typically very quiet, decent and loves God. Elijah was surprised when the husband said to him, "Please, bail me out! For more than five, my wife has turned down every sexual advance. She never would allow me touch her without an apology for a wrong that I committed against her months ago. I have forgotten the scenario and what I did, but she has managed to hold it against me anyway.

Tracy went to Elijah, and there she made that statements:

"Unless he tells me sorry, I am not going to have him touch me again. I can no longer put up with his unkind acts anymore. I have forgiven him several times, but for this, I will never let go. He must apologize or never."

"And what was it that John did," he asked.

"He treats me like a slave! He comes home and demands constantly, he has no consideration for the milestones that I might be trying to meet, or the status of the kids. Being home with two children, homeschooling, and running a home-based business is not easy! Besides, he does not give me nearly as much as I give him. He goes to work and brings home money. It should be 50/50, but it seems like it is just me giving, giving, and giving all the time!

The 50/50 syndrome

There is this school of thought that believes that marriage is a 50/50 thing. That means I give 50% of myself and resources to the family while my spouse does the same. That is a lie from the pit of hell. There is no 50/50 program for your marriage but only a 100/100. Give 100%! Compromise is necessary for conflict resolution, but not for commitment. Compromise requires give and take. Marriage commitment is a 100% investment! Drop the 50/50 mentality because it has no place in your commitment with your spouse! Give without expectation, which is true love. You are here to give, give and give, even if you never receive. But the truth is that whatever a person sows that shall he also reap. The law of sowing and reaping will and must catch up with you if you in to give. You will have nothing to lose in the long run but everything to gain.

The Gender-Cultural syndrome

We have one culture; it is the Bible, the Word of God. "To him that knows to do good and does not do it, to him it is sin." [17]. Cultural gender expectations must be discussed, agreements must be made, and accommodations to make those things possible have to be set in place.

My husband had a cultural gender expectation that I would cook daily because his mom did. I was a mom, wife; I worked full-time, was in school and arrived home between 4-6 PM. We discussed the expectation, neither of us had a problem with fulfilling it, but I requested that he pick up our son and help with keeping the kitchen clean, so the job is not overwhelming for me with limited time. We agreed. When he picked up our son, I would get home between 3-5 PM and the kitchen was ready for me to cook. This enabled me to have more time to cook, and fulfill our families' expectation.

Who said you cannot reach a common ground with your spouse in the running of your home? You must understand that culture is not what will run your home for you, but UNDERSTANDING. My number one mentor, the Holy Spirit defined understanding for me with respect to marriage as "COMPROMISE." You have to learn the act of compromise. You have to shift grounds until you reach a place and a state where there is a win/win for both parties. Hey, she is your wife, and not your slave. He is your husband, not your client.

---

17 James 4:17

Summary

- Drop The Conditions - Example: "I cannot love him if he does not apologize" "I cannot love him if he eats my leftover food and leaves me none", "I cannot love her if he raises his voice", "I cannot love her if she doesn't cook", I cannot love him if he doesn't cut the grass"

- Give 100%! Drop the 50/50 mentality! Give without expectation which is true love

- Cultural gender expectations must be discussed, agreements must be made, and accommodations to make those things possible have to be set in place

Exercise

Decide on a matter that needs your compromise. Examine what your spouse was requesting, and see how you can compromise more for a solution.

CHAPTER TEN

ALLY WITH POWER TEAMS

"Teamwork is the ability to work together toward a common vision. The ability to direct individual accomplishments toward organizational objectives. It is the fuel that allows common people to attain uncommon results."

— Andrew Carnegie

You should maintain a team of people that can help you break the wind (obstacles) that come against your marriage. People that can love your love, and want it to last forever.

The Story Of Gary And "The Street Life"

Gary grew up in an underprivileged neighborhood. Three generations of his family were groomed in the area of lowest income and highest criminal activity in New York City. Growing up, Gary was taught how to sell drugs to make a living, he became one of the most well-known drug dealers, and at 450 pounds with the ability to lift twice his weight, he was a fierce opponent if anyone tried to defy him. Not only was he a fierce opponent, but his group of close knit allies were willing to fight to death to support Gary. If you said that you had association with Gary, everyone in the neighborhood either pledged loyalty or turned their backs out of the fear of repercussion.

After ten years living the "street life", Gary lost his closest friend to heart disease. The death hit Gary very hard; nothing in life made him feel the agony that he felt inside as a result of the loss of his closest friend.

At the funeral, the Pastor preached about life purpose. He said, "You have been sent to this Earth for a reason, and generations of people can be transformed by your actions: good or bad". Gary was really touched by the message and decided to align his life with the purpose of God. He accepted Jesus as his Lord and Savior, and abandoned the drug selling business.

Six months after his conversion, Gary spotted the woman of his dreams, Pam. She was a ministry leader and a world-renowned speaker. She could see that Gary had a powerful call on his life, but knew that he needed to abandon his friends to improve. She was very attracted to him, their first conversation was breathtaking, and she believed that he was "the one". Pam married Gary and their love ignited. He got heavily involved in ministry, they would travel the world ministering together, and the ministry leaders would give him great ideas to increase their love.

Gary still had an extreme loyalty to his street friends, and they still wanted to be around him. He would fly from his ministry and his wife quarterly to go and spend time with his friends from "the hood". They would smoke, drink, and fight together as he did before he met Jesus. Gary had a difficult time acting in what seemed as disloyalty for his friends that were willing to put their lives down to support him. They each had several women that they spoke highly of "hitting and running", and they encouraged him to do the same. "I understand that she seems to be working well for you, man, but you remember all the women who seemed like they had it all together growing up? They all turned out rotten! You better get you a little backup", his friends would say.

He desired to make more of his life, but it was very difficult for him to transform while he continued to go back to a contaminated mentality. Furthermore, it was nearly impossible for his friends to understand the purpose in making the same decision as Gary when his life appeared identical when he was with them.

Though, we cannot rule out the place of fraternity and fellowship, it is still important to define the limits of our involvement with other people and also to state the particular kind of association we should keep.

Keep close to Couples with infectious love

If you want to keep your love thermometer high and warm, stay around couples with infectious love. We had said in an earlier chapter that love is infectious, you can catch it, and since it when you come into an environment where it exists. Love is contagious. And love epidemic is the only one that I know never to kill. Catch it! Be infested with love!

You will know couples who have this infectious love by the words that they use to describe one another, the way they smile when they look each other in the eyes, the priority that they hold their marriage, and the boundaries that they hold for each other. Find friends with infectious love, so that when you do encounter obstacles, you can be encouraged to persist.

Limit your environment of marriage conflicts and resolving conflicts

For Gary, he continued to explore life in his previous reality. He had since realized that he can thrive with a loving wife and a different career, but he continued to return to the old lifestyle, and receive the same advice.

If you want your marriage to work, it will be friends and life-styles that you must avoid. Anyone or anything that does not encourage you to have a better marriage is territory that you should avoid. Your friends and family should be advising you how to please your husband or wife as supported by scripture, they should not be advising you to entertain adulterous relation-ships, explore media that may be confrontational, or participate in business affairs that may cause disagreement. Teamwork is your goal in marriage! Your spouse is your team; no one else is a lifelong teammate by divine agreement aside from your spouse (not even your parents).

Everybody should not know come into your marriage and life. There are some people that should never know that you have quarrels to settle with your spouse. Assign who comes to talk to you about conflict resolution in your home and who does not.

The Bible specifies who should handle conflicts for Christ fol-lowers. Paul said:

"If any of you has a dispute with another, do you dare to take it before the ungodly for judgment instead of before the Lord's people? Or do you not know that the Lord's people will judge the world? And if you are to judge the world, are you not competent to judge trivial cases? Do you not know that we will judge angels? How much more the things of this life! Therefore, if you have disputes about such matters, do you ask for a ruling from those whose way of life is scorned in the church? I say this to shame you. Is it possible that there is nobody among you wise enough to judge a dispute between believers? But instead, one brother takes another to court—and this in front of unbelievers!"

Take your most stubborn disputes to wise men and women who know how to make a marriage work and know how to conceal a matter. If you have witnessed leaders who are gossipers and share other people's personal matters, you should not disclose the sacred matters of your marriage to them. Rather, you should only disclose your information for solutions, and to those whom you are assured will pray, fast, and ally with you in spiritual warfare. Others who do not possess the spiritual maturity to encourage your relationship, should be exempted from hearing your personal matters.

Then stay inspired to love more and better

Nothing could be sadder than a marriage that has lost its flame and inspiration! That is like hell on earth. Why not invent ways and ideas that are peculiar to you to keep the flame of your marriage vows. Be a creative, innovative lover. To love is work, so work at working it with novelty as the case may be.

Think of adventures that could spark your interest, sign them up for a course that they have been dreaming of taking, cook meals that are different from the norm, wear clothes that can turn up the heat, take on a responsibility around the house that would typically be burdensome to your spouse; all these things should be done without regard to the effort that you receive. Igniting change can keep you both guessing, and add excitement to your marriage.

Summary

- Ally With Power Teams
- Stay around couples with infectious love
- Limit your environment of marriage conflicts and resolving conflicts
- Stay inspired to love more and better

Exercise

Take some time to pray about the people that you will meet this year. Pray that you would be alert and notice God's assignment for the people that cross your path this year. Pray that you have the courage to let go when counterfeits come. Pray about it and let God guide you to establish new relationships. Understand that relationship is everything.

CHAPTER ELEVEN

BE EQUAL

"Raise your words, not voice. It is rain that grows flowers, not thunder."

— Rumi

All over the world today, there is the clamor for gender equality, women's liberation and equal societal rights and values. As if the world just woke up and are trying to catch up with God. The Bible has never been silenced on this matter. He who made them at the beginning, made them male and female. Even the serpent who tempted them at the beginning of creation to fall, tempted them male and female. And He who redeemed them about 2000 years ago, redeemed them male and female. Are we just waking up? No matter how late we come out of our slumber, it is better than not waking up at all.

The Story Of Bob And Georgia

Bob and Georgia were just recently married. They are both in the late 40s, and were eager to have the companionship of marriage. They courted for six months prior to their marriage, and traveled all around the world together. They had a magnificent time in their courting.

Bob is the Mayor of a small town. He has served as mayor for 35+ years, and keeps being nominated by the voters to serve again.

Georgia is a judge in her city council. Georgia presides over several cases daily and has high esteem for making very fair judgements.

Bob and Georgia have been married and living together for two months and they are beginning to have conflicts. Bob wants Georgia to cut his toenails and wash his feet weekly. He does not feel that women should handle money, so he wants to take away Georgia's access to all of their banking accounts.

Georgia, on the other hand, feels that Bob is lazy because he will not cut the grass. She presides over cases all day, and always had a maid clean and cook dinner. Now, Bob wants her to perform these domestic tasks, and she is dissatisfied with their teamwork in the home responsibilities. Their home is completely disrupted.

Treat each partner as a valued asset; a body part of yours

Both you and your spouse have perceptions, desires, interests, assets, and achievements. Household tasks are the responsibility of every resident regardless of where you live. As a single person, you must handle responsibilities regardless of sex, ethnic background, age, culture, and any other forms of division. Everyone has household responsibilities! Couples must divide the household responsibilities in a way that both are willing to cooperate.

One person should not be placing demands that they see their spouse is completely in opposition to, or they have no interest in maintaining a happy marriage. For the sake of peace, you must decide what each of you are willing to be responsible for, and perform those tasks.

Previously, we spoke of consideration and being aware of your spouse's physiological status. Household responsibilities can also be a stimulus to stress. If you are able, assist your spouse as much as possible. Increase your teamwork. Treat your spouse as your own body. Do not demand things out of pride.

How would you want to treat your body? The day you married that woman whether you are higher or lower paid than she is notwithstanding, you became equal with her, and you became one.

You are equal; see it that way. The woman was taken from the man's side and not from his toe. Does that say something to you? That is a fact that you must understand, embrace and celebrate. Love lifts us to its level. One with Christ, joint heirs with him …; for he that joined to the Lord is one spirit with him. And He is not ashamed to call us brethren.[18] Does it offend Jesus that He has lifted and elevated you to his level as co heirs of the grace of God, seated with him in heavenly places? You must wake up if you are fighting for superiority. Wake up! Keep pride, hatred, and dissensions out. Keep it in perspective, let there be mutual respect but not pride, hate nor dissension.

Summary

- Be Equal
- Treat each partner as a valued asset; a body part of yours
- Keep pride, hatred, and dissensions out

---

18   1 Cor.6:17 and Heb. 2:11

Exercise

Meditate on how you can break down walls of division and inequality within your home. Ask God, "How can my husband and I be more united in our views of one another? Let your Kingdom come in our marriage now."

CHAPTER TWELVE

TALK TO GOD

"The battle for our lives, and the lives and souls of our children,
our husbands, our friends, our families, our neighbors, and
our nation is waged on our knees. When we don't pray, it's like
sitting on the sidelines watching those we love and care about
scrambling through a war zone, getting shot at from every angle.
When we do pray, however, we're in the battle alongside them,
approaching God's power on their behalf. If we also declare the
Word of God in our prayers, then we wield a powerful weapon
against which no enemy can prevail."

— Stormie Omartian, *The Power of a Praying Woman Bible:
Prayer and Study Helps*

I want to quickly inform you that this chapter is the lifeblood
of this book. Life is spiritual. Spiritual forces are more real and
more powerful than physical forces. Marriage is spiritual. Sex
is spiritual. So you have been dealing with spiritual verities all the
while.

Your coming together in marriage is not by chance but by the
invisible unseen forces that have been guiding you even from your
mother's womb. Did you ever ask yourself, "Of all of the families
that I could have been born, why was I born of this family?" Why
your mother? Why not someone else's? You couldn't have determined that, but God alone did. And that's the same way He did
your marriage to the man or woman you call your "spouse". He

has not stopped guiding you. Now, what are you going to do to complement what destiny has started?

The Story Of Joyce

"I love to pray and I did pray" said Joyce to one of her neighbors. "But I don't enjoy praying with my husband. I believe my quiet time should be between me and God alone. Why must my husband and I pray together? I was not raised that way. In my family everyone does their praying, no one disturbing the other.

Everyone knows what they want God to do for them and they go ask God for it on their own. More so, each one has their personal problems and should not be bothered by someone else's. Christianity is personal. Salvation is personal. I will give account of my life to God and my husband will give his. So what does it matter if we pray together. He is serving his God and I am serving mine." Joyce complained angrily to her friend and neighbor.

You should not still think in terms of being single and selfish. Now you are two and you must begin to do things together. What God has joined together, let no man, or foolishness separate. And the two shall become one… So in what ways are you supposed to walk and work together:

To implement Spiritual Disciplines Together (when equally yoked)

When believers try to impose religion on unbelievers or those exploring, it usually increases resistance. For unequally yoked couples, the party that is following Christ, must seek the Kingdom regarding their spouse and family. The battle is strictly spiritual thru prayer, fasting, and worship rather than talking, arguing, and manipulating. Talk to God about what you should say, what you should do, and how to persevere when things are not equal.

Now, for the Christ followers:

Set aside time together to pray, fast and to seek the face of God. For us in our family, we have sanctified the first activity of the morning for daily Bible Study and prayer, we pray in the evenings before bed, and we sanctify Sundays for God.

If you are one who believes in going for retreats or solitary places like mountains and camps for prayers, why not? "For one will chase a thousand but two will put ten thousand to flight.".[19] Don't underestimate the power of two in the realm of the spirit. Heaven shakes when two united spirits pray.

Prayer is the creative tool that we use to manifest heavenly things. If you desire to manifest change in your marriage, go to the Spirit! Create the change in the spiritual realm thru prayer, and assuredly, it will manifest on Earth!

In Praying For your spouse

I know of women who vowed they will not stop praying until they see their husbands become what God has made them to be. Thank God for women. I have seen and read of women who through prayer and fasting, moved their husbands into their God ordained destinies. You have not prayed until you make your spouse a priority in your prayers. When you have questions and things that you do not understand, pray. You may not understand

---

19 Joshua 23:10, Deut 32:30, and Mat. 18:19

your spouse all of the time, but assuredly, God does. Do not allow the Kingdom of Darkness to take away your marriage. Thru prayer, meditation, and spiritual warfare, you must be aggressive and fight back! Pray for him! Pray for her!

Meditate on how they can be free from their obstacles

Take the time as a husband or as a wife to think through how your spouse could overcome obstacles. There is this saying: The person who watches a soccer match sees the errors of the player more than himself. It is the one who observes, that notices the mistakes of the person being observed.

So take the time to observe your spouse and then to think about how he or she can overcome those obstacles. You are set up by God to help him or her succeed. Do this with love and tenderness. Nobody can turn down love even when it is rebuke.

Forgive immediately and daily to ensure access to the heavens

"And whenever you stand praying, if you have anything against anyone, forgive him... that your prayer will not be hindered.[20] As I said previously, forgiveness is an act of divinity. It is a requirement of every living being. There is no perfection under the sun, and if you hold unforgiveness towards someone, this inhibits your prayer from being answered. Forgive, so that your prayers can be heard!

---

20 Mark 11:25 and 1 Pet. 3:7

Summary

- Talk To God
- Implement Spiritual Disciplines Together (when equally yoked)
- Implement Spiritual Disciplines in Private
- Intercede For Your Spouse and their Affairs
- Pray For your spouse
- Meditate on how they can be free from their obstacles
- Forgive immediately and daily to ensure access to the heavens

THE DIVINE COMMISSION FOR YOUR WORLD-CLASS MARRIAGE

I trust that you have enjoyed reading thru this book and you have gained insight for how you can achieve a world-class marriage. Joy and peace are your inheritance! God created man and woman in His image. Do you think that God ever has conflict? No! He mourns for you in your turmoil, but He does not experience conflict of His own; He conquers! He is too abundant with solutions to marinate in problems, and He desires for your marriage to be a recipient of His solution-focused Kingdom. He created you to experience the abundance as He does. Meditate on the words of scripture, the laws written in this book, the exercises that you completed, and invite the Holy Spirit into your presence. He will be the closest companion that you can ever know; closer than a spouse, child, sibling, parent, mentor, or best friend. He will lead you thru every trial, obstacle, or conflict that you may have in your marriage, and guide you to a world-class, world revered marriage.

A biblical affirmation to repeat in times where assurance of His presence is needed:

The LORD is my shepherd. I am never in need. He leads me beside peaceful waters. He guides me along the paths of righteousness for the sake of his name. Even though I walk through the dark valley of death,   because you are with me, I fear no harm. Your rod and your staff give me courage. You prepare a banquet for me while my enemies watch. You anoint my head with oil. My cup overflows. Certainly, goodness and mercy will stay close to me all the days of my life, and I will remain in the Lord's house for days without end.

-Psalms 23, NIV, Written by King David

May the Kingdom of God be manifested in and thru your marriage now!

— **Tiffany Domena**

ABOUT THE AUTHOR

Tiffany Domena is an Ambassador of the Kingdom of Heaven, wife, mother, bestselling author, and advocate for living your life by YHWH's design. Bringing nine years of military experience, an educational background in Bible (Bachelor's in Religion along with some graduate coursework), and a Biblical worldview, Tiffany enjoys training others on how to be successful in their deployments to the Earth. She is the founder at Kingdom of Heaven Ambassadors International where her primary focus is taking enemy territory back on the internet and in mainstream media, and refocusing hearts and minds on Yeshua the Messiah. Expertly publishing ten books, hosting a podcast, and blogging on pertinent topics that strike our world, Tiffany's passion bleeds thru her work, and encourages those who get wind of her. She has been known to speak and write on topics including prayer, life purpose, marriage, sex, temptation, goal-setting, wisdom, and prosperity. Other books by Tiffany include:

- 12 Undeniable Laws For Being Wise As A Snake

- 12 Undeniable Laws For Prayer

- 12 Undeniable Laws For Sex

- 12 Undeniable Laws For Being A Kingdom of Heaven Ambassador

- 12 Undeniable Laws For Prosperity

- Perception: The World's Most Affluent Leader and companion workbook

- Transform Your Habits To Create Your Position of Power Workbook

- Someone Covets You

Find more resources, training, or to subscribe to Tiffany's blog, podcast, or social network, visit www.kingdomofheavenambassador.com

ONE LAST THING...

If you enjoyed this book, I would love to hear! I personally read all reviews written on my books, and I use them to make the books better and more effective. I would greatly appreciate your feedback at the links below:

Amazon Link:

http://www.amazon.com/Tiffany-Domena/e/B00MSHE0LI

Website Link:

http://www.kingdomofheavenambassador.com/shop/

Goodreads Link:

https://www.goodreads.com/author/show/8459952.Tiffany_Domena

May God bless you!

Tiffany Domena